Heartfelt

Heartfelt

Make
every day
count